What others are saying about April Stutzman and Gateway to my Miracle

April's book, **Gateway To My Miracle**, is a very transparent testimony of her upbringing. She shares how the Lord brought her through, even though she had no idea it was Him at that time. This story will inspire others to "not give up" but to believe God's Word that we can look to Him to use our past to shape us & prepare us for His Call & Destiny on our lives. You will gain helpful "tools for life" as you read April's story. Be Blessed & empowered.

Constance J Bounds

God's Eagles Ministry

April is a Holy Ghost filled women of God with compassion for others through the Love of Jesus Christ. This book will ignite your Faith, Transform your life, bring deliverance, and set you ablaze for Jesus. These Holy Spirit inspired words to come deep from the heart.

Patricia Doty

Pastor/Evangelist

April Stutzman is not your ordinary minister of the gospel. She is a prophetess with a special forces mantle. She knows how to live from our heavenly places in Christ Jesus. In this book, you will learn how to receive supernatural keys from God and impart them to your earthly circumstances. These keys have been given to her by Jesus and will cause the earth to align itself with the Kingdom of Heaven. As you are reading this book, pray for God to impart these *divine keys and strategies* into your life, your family, and your church and watch the kingdom of Heaven come to earth and create lasting change.

Apostle Clinton C. Baker Co-Founder of Valiant Ministries International, Inc.

This book is an incredible testimony of God's faithfulness to heal and deliver us from a life of misery and pain! I read it cover to cover on a plane ride and was very moved by the powerful declarations and healing that took place! April is a powerful prophetic voice, and her story of redemption is fantastic!

Beth Packard

In this book, April talks about her journey of healing, both inner healing and miraculous healing from fibromyalgia. I had heard a podcast interview with April, and from her brief testimony I heard, I knew I had to read this book. The book did not disappoint. A few quotes from the book that resonated with me. I needed inner healing and deliverance. Why was this not being talked about and taught?" "There was a wound in my soul, and deliverance was needed. Oh, how I wish the church would talk about this stuff and allow the Holy Spirit to make people whole." "A person can only love at the level their heart has received healing and love from God." And then when God healed her from fibromyalgia, she heard God say: "If I can heal the nations, what kind of God would I be if I didn't heal you?"

Joanna M. Russell

Gateway to My Miracle is April Stutzman's powerful testimony of Christ's redeeming love and miraculous power! As you read, April walks you through her own personal journey into healing and freedom. Her words ordained by Heaven and revelation from the Father will help set you free from the lies of the enemy, past trauma, and physical pain. If you are in need of keys for breakthroughs in your own life, then this is the book for you. As April shares her own emotional wounds of the past and infirmity, it will open your eyes and awaken your heart to the deep and hidden things in your own soul that Jesus wants to heal and deliver you from. This book had me searching my own heart as I read it. Get ready to unlock the gateway to the Miracle you have been praying for!

Teryn Yancey

Co-founder of Glory Culture International

I loved this book. Her testimony is amazing. Her healing and journey with God are exciting to read about. I have already read it twice. Easy to understand and receive your own miracles.

Sherry Boyd

Gateway

to my

Miracle

Gateway
to my
Miracle

April Stutzman

Copyright © 2018, 2020 by April Stutzman

Imprint: Independently published

Printed in the United States of America

All rights reserved. "No part of this publication may be reproduced, distributed, or transmitted in any form or by any means, including photocopying, recording, or other electronic or mechanical methods, or by any information storage and retrieval system without the prior written permission of the publisher, except in the case of very brief quotations embodied in critical reviews and certain other noncommercial uses permitted by copyright law."

First Printing: 2018

Second Edition Published: 2020

ISBN: 13-978-1-7351751-9-5

Library of Congress Control Number: 2020915891

Library of Congress Cataloging-in-Publication Data is on file at the Library of Congress, Washington, DC.

Audible: Audible, Amazon, and Itunes and other platform's

Cover design by Amazing_design5 with Fiverr

Photos: shutterstock, canva, unsplash, and pixabay

Unless otherwise noted, Scripture quotations are from the NET Bible® copyright ©1996-2006 by Biblical Studies Press, L.L.C. http://netbible.com All rights reserved.

Scripture quotations marked (NIV) are taken from the Holy Bible, New International Version®, NIV®. Copyright © 1973, 1978, 1984, 2011 by Biblica, Inc.™ Used by permission of Zondervan.

Scripture taken from the New King James Version®. Copyright © 1982 by Thomas Nelson. Used by permission. All rights reserved.

Scripture quotations marked (NIV) are taken from the Holy Bible, New International Version®, NIV®. Copyright © 1973, 1978, 1984, 2011 by Biblica, Inc.® Used by permission of Zondervan. All rights are reserved worldwide. www.zondervan.com The "NIV" and "New International Version" are trademarks registered in the United States Patent and Trademark Office by Biblica, Inc.®

Dedication

I dedicate this book to the **Holy Spirit**. He is a person, and I honor Him. I would not be where I am today if He had not cooperated with what the Father wanted for me, and supernaturally healed the wounds of my soul. I owe You my life, Holy Spirit, and I say thank you! You're the lover of my soul.

To my **husband, Richard,** who is the love of my life and has believed and supported me since day one. I am so thankful for your support daily and to be able to move with the Holy Spirit as you cheer me on! You're my best friend. Thank you, Jesus, for bringing us together. One of the best days of my life was when I married you.

To my **kids,** whom I love with all my heart. As I stand back and watch the Lord restore the years that the enemy has stolen from us, may my ceiling be your floor!

Contents

Foreword 13

Introduction 15

Struggling for Identity 19

Overcoming Trauma 29

Yearning for God 37

The Process 47

Walking in Wholeness 59

From Victim to Victory 71

Closing Thoughts 73

    Chapter One Notes………………………………..75

    Chapter Two Notes………………………………..77

    Chapter Three Notes………………………………79

    Chapter Four Notes………………………………..81

    Chapter Five Notes………………………………..83

    Chapter Six Notes…………………………………85

Notes…………………………………………………..87

About the Author……………………………………..89

    Prayer for Impartation……………………………127

    Invite April to Speak at your Next Event………..129

Foreword

Gateway To My Miracle is the powerful testimony of April Stutzman's personal journey to healing. Far more than just the transparent sharing of a life-changing testimony, ***Gateway To My Miracle*** boldly addresses questions and misconceptions that surface in the body of Christ as well as outside of the church. She points out the lack of teaching and understanding regarding these subjects and how difficult it often is for people to receive help when they need it. Out of sheer desperation and a hunger for the truth, April sought out answers to address the overwhelming problems she personally faced problems that the doctors had no cure for. Her experience in the medical field brings further credibility and knowledge to her experiences.

April's teaching stems from a heart of compassion and a desire for all people to experience healing and deliverance. Her teaching style is direct and to the point, revealing lies and pointing to the truth—truths she applied to her own life in order to experience freedom! Her powerful testimony, coupled with the power of God as she applies the breaker anointing to demolish the lies of the enemy, brings freedom and releases people from bondage.

Whether you are experiencing the need for physical or emotional healing yourself or are taking up the mantle to battle for others, you will find that this book a faith builder and a powerful resource. This book will greatly benefit both you and those you care about. May God increase your faith and give you victory!

Jodi Ferguson

Co-Founder/Co-Director Warriors Heart Ministry

Women's Equipping Network Producer of TV Show, Signs Following with JC

Introduction

Does God care about my pain? Is He a personal God? Even if my pain is not seen on the outside, does He care about the pain inside of me? Can He help me? Is there hope for me? Why do I keep struggling with the same things over and over again in my life? Why do I not seem to be as effective as the people around me? If you have ever asked yourself these questions, this is the book for you. Are you longing to see changes in your life and in your health?

This is the story of how God changed me from the inside out and transformed my life physically and emotionally.

As I lay sick in my bed, I wondered how my life could go on. Questions kept coming to me: Does God heal today? Was I being judged for some mistake? These questions kept hitting my mind. Bad theology crowded my mind and my thoughts. I needed healing, and I needed a breakthrough NOW! Why was I not seeing people healed in the churches that I visited during this time? I was left with a lot of confusion on the subject of healing. If the subject was talked about in a church service, it was very brief, and healing was not demonstrated. I would look around, glancing over the people in the church I was attending, and I'd see half the church was sick.

I quickly developed an interest in healing and began to study this subject. I did not know where to turn or what to do. So, I started crying out to the Lord for answers. The verse that kept coming to me was: "The thief comes only to steal and kill and destroy; I [Jesus] have come so that they may have life, and may have it abundantly." (John 10:10, NET) I was not experiencing this verse. I knew that if it was in the Bible, I wanted to experience it! I wanted an abundant life. Sickness was robbing me of time with my children. Frequently, verses like Jeremiah 29:11-13 would pop up in my mind. No matter what religion was telling me, something in my Spirit said my life is not lining up with the Scriptures, so there must be more.

Some of the things I was told about healing made no sense to me. For example: "The third Monday of the month, if God is in a good mood, and if He feels like healing you, then it has to be a sovereign thing, and you just wake up healed." As a single mom with three kids, I needed to be able to function. I was at the point of being bedridden on my days off, and the doctor had put me on part-time work because I had been diagnosed with what the world would call fibromyalgia. If Jesus heals today, how come no one around me was talking about it? I had attended church most of my life but had seen very few healings and miracles, and I always thought this was strange.

How would I get my breakthrough? Did God care that my children and I were suffering? I felt alone, unsure, and scared. I couldn't sleep at night because the pain was so great. On top of that, I was breastfeeding every two and a half hours each night. Have you ever asked any of these questions? Have you ever been in need of an immediate breakthrough? Have you ever felt alone and unsure of the future?

Jesus is the same yesterday, today, and forever! Keep turning the pages of this book and see what God will do. I believe that through sharing my own story, you will find keys to unlock the gateway to your own Miracle.

I would love to have you join me in a simple prayer. You don't have to say the prayer—nobody will know if you do or if you don't, except for Jesus. Even in your sickbed, He hears you, He cares for you, and He sees your suffering. Take my hand and be brave. I believe in you!

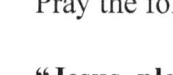

Pray the following:

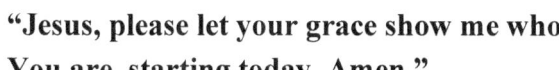

"Jesus, please let your grace show me who You are, starting today. Amen."

One simple prayer; one simple invitation. He will meet you in your most profound need. Don't be afraid!

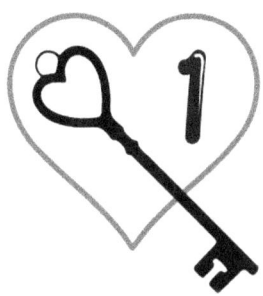

Struggling for Identity

"A person can only love at the level their heart has received healing and love from God."

As a very young child, I struggled with my identity. I remember being six years old, and my parents were divorcing. I felt like I was lost. The trauma of it all and a voice of accusation hit me, lying to me, saying: "It's your fault." I did not know at that age that I did not have to receive those words. These were lies of the enemy. But I remember crying, day after day, wondering where my daddy was, and why he couldn't be with me. Fear attacked me when my father first left. After this, he was in an accident at work. He cut his hand and was unable to work due to his injury. During this time, I was not able to see him, and my heart yearned, day after day, for my dad.

Looking back, I wish I had cried out to my heavenly Father to take the pain away and comfort me. The "father wound" was fresh in my life.

As you read this if you can identify with this pain, ask the Holy Spirit to heal the father wound in your heart.

I declare over you:

I declare that you do not carry an orphan spirit, but a spirit of adoption from your heavenly Father. You are His son or His daughter. I thank the Lord that your identity is established in Him.

We lived next door to my grandmother, so I would run over to her house for homemade gravy and all of the comforts that a grandmother can offer. Visiting with her was the best way for me to escape what was going on with my emotions. It was my safe haven. The Lord was drawing me in, and He was using my grandmother to do it.

She attended a little Methodist church down the road, and she would take me with her. I thought it was cool because they had snack time, and the Lord's house was filled with cookies and sweets. It seemed like all the church members loved to bake, and, of course, kids love sugar! I look back now and laugh, but it worked, and I kept going to church every week. If I went, I knew I could have snacks, and these were the good ones!

There was a generous spread of homemade pies, cakes, and you name it—it was there. But as I kept attending, I began to wonder, "Who is God, and does He love me? Is he someone who is distant, or could I hear His voice as Moses did?"

I remember being amazed as they used the Velcro boards with the Bible characters to teach me the story of Moses. I was amazed that God would help one man that much, so I continued going—for the snacks, the crafts, and vacation Bible school. It helped to take my mind off things at home. I was begging to know whether there really is a God and if I could accept Him. I just wasn't sure how. I noticed that year after year, as I kept going to church, I became more and more hungry to know this God that they would preach and teach about. Could I find this God? Would He love me? These were all questions I would ask myself in my heart day after day.

Next came a chapter of my life that I was not prepared for. My mom got remarried, and my dad did as well. Both happened at about the same time. Soon afterward, it was announced that I would have a new sibling on each side. Well, as a child with a childish nature, and not God's nature, I was mad! How could God let this happen? I had just started seeing my dad again, and now there was going to be a new baby! What in the world…? Due to my own wounds, I was not happy, but rather jealous. Little did I know that, in my own home, we would experience abuse as well.

At first, I was controlled in very small ways, such as being put down for everything I did. My mom also began to experience emotional abuse. There was a lot of anger and rage in the house, and I didn't know how to defend my mother. Fear started to develop. It's funny how fear gets a grip on your soul slowly, and it can go unnoticed. There were violent outbursts towards my mom, and I would cry in my bedroom, not knowing how to handle this.

My young, wounded heart could not take anything else. I remember attending a support group for children of divorced parents, but no one talked about abuse. Therefore, I didn't understand what was going on. Was this abuse? Was this normal in a family? I had no idea. I was hit with confusion because of what was going on. It felt like my whole life had flipped upside down. At the same time, I was wondering if there is a God and how I could find him.

At this point, I was also dealing with shame because I couldn't understand why this was happening to me. Was there something wrong with me? Feelings of rejection set in without me realizing it; it was very subtle and deceiving. My plan was to stay at my grandmother's house as much as I could, so I could feel safe. I didn't know what else to do, or whom to tell. I did not realize that trauma had set in, and probably posttraumatic stress disorder (PTSD) as well.

Then, one night, things escalated. Really late that night, I was trying to go to bed. I had been isolated in my room and was only allowed to come out to eat. My stepdad would make me stay in my room, and I was not allowed to spend much time with my mom or little brother. Even though I lived in the same house with them, I was so lonely because I could only come out when he allowed me to. I could read or watch TV, but that's all there was to do in my room. Back in those days, we did not have video games or iPads, and kids didn't have cell phones. I think this was when depression set in. I questioned where God was while this was happening to my family. Did He love me or even cares about what was happening under our roof?

Finally, it all spilled out at school. I got a D on my report card and was terrified to go home. I told the school principal that I was afraid to go home because my step-dad might beat me. Then something happened that was really confusing. While I was being held at the school, when they were contacting my mom, my step-dad sent flowers to me at the school, denying everything. I was in shock. I was mad! I didn't want the stupid flowers; I wanted him to stop abusing my family and me. I wanted to not have to fear my home environment and not have someone control every single part of my day.

Things eased up at the house for a while, but not for long. I was hoping that the attention from the school would change things and that we would have a normal family again. But it didn't stop. Soon after, my stepdad went back to treating everyone in my family the same way. I was becoming more and more afraid, and could not sleep at night. I didn't know the Spirit of fear was becoming a stronghold in my life at that time.

Have you been through something traumatic? Do you often feel fearful?

Say this prayer with me:

"Lord, I renounce the Spirit of fear, and I declare Your love is made perfect in me, and that's my portion. Thank You that Your angels are protecting me."

I realize now that this Spirit of fear was trying to shut down a gift the Lord had given me, called "seeing in the spirit." But that's a subject for another book.

I wish I could say it got better from that point on. It did not. There was one night when my step-dad handcuffed my mother to the bed, and all I could hear was my mom screaming, "Somebody helps me!" I stood paralyzed in my bed. What was I to do? It was dark outside, and, if I jumped out my window to get help, I could get hurt. The screaming finally stopped, but I think I was up most of the night. I am not sure why I didn't talk to my mom the next day. I think denial is sometimes easier. I also did not know what to say. At the age of seven years old, I didn't realize how bizarre and abnormal this behavior really was.

I longed for my real dad. Every now and then, I would get to see him, but he drank a lot and was very poor. He was trying to make a living, and it was a long drive for him to come to get me. I remember bawling one time because he was one minute late to pick me up, and then my stepdad would not let me go with my dad. A spirit of control was operating with full force, and I now know that, when control operates, it releases witchcraft. We are not designed to control other human beings. I hadn't been able to see my birth dad for months, and my stepdad made him leave. This is not meant to be a scenario to bash my dad. My dad had his own set of wounds that were very great, and, at my immature age, I had no idea what he had been through. A person can only love at the level their heart has received healing and love from God. My dad had been abused and traumatized on many levels, but I would not find out about this until I was much older.

Some of my fondest memories were when I got to go visit my dad, and we spent time together. He would make it special. He would wake up and make Hoe Cake. Does anyone remember that? Basically, it was a poor man's bread recipe: all ingredients were thrown together in a long pan that looked like cornbread. He would make me sausages and gravy, and I loved it! Just the fact that he did that for me made me feel so special. One year, I remember he used all his extra money and went out to buy me a Nintendo game, some fancy pens, some paper, and a duck pencil sharpener. I was in Heaven! That pencil sharpener was so unique. To this day, that gift still touches my heart, because he used every dime he had to get it for me.

We would play that Nintendo until we beat Mario 3—one of my best memories! Spending a day with my dad playing that video game was a special treat because it was something we could do together and with a common goal. But then reality would hit, and I would have to go home and face my normal life. I was not able to see my dad very often; sometimes, it was only once every six months.

Much to my surprise, I quickly got over being jealous when I found out my baby brother was to be born. I was so excited and naively thought this would change the dynamics of my family. Surely my stepdad would be gentle and respectful to a baby. It was something positive to focus on. I am sorry to say that things went downhill fast.

My little brother was born, and he was perfect. I remember staring at him while he was sleeping and thinking about how amazing he was. But then the abuse started on the baby, and I did not know how to handle this situation either. He would cry, and my stepdad would cover his face with a pillow as he screamed. I had no awareness of what to do, thinking, "My God, I hope he doesn't kill him." He would shake my brother when he screamed, saying, "Do you want him? Do you want him?" I thought he was going to throw the baby at me. Many years down the road, God had to heal me of false guilt. I took it as my responsibility to protect my brother, and, in my mind, I had failed to do so. It was many years later, in my adult life, that God had to reach down and pull all the infection out of my soul. He helped me to realize that it was not my job to protect my brother; I was just a kid.

I did not realize that the enemy was coming hard and fast at my family, but what Satan uses for evil, God turns around and

Struggling for Identity

uses for good. "And we know that all things work together for good for those who love God, who are called according to his purpose. (Romans 8:28, NET) You see, there is an assignment of evil spirits on trauma because the enemy is terrified of who you are and of your assignment on the earth from God. Therefore, he tries to take you out by keeping you from developing into the son or daughter of the living God that you really are. BE BOLD! I declare you will recover everything! All this evil that was done to me had the opposite effect on me. Satan thought he would make me quit, but, instead, it gave me GRIT! The hardships created a deep hunger in me, and a thirst to know the living God of the universe. It made me cry out for God all the more.

I started asking more and more questions, trying to figure out the character and nature of God. I did not realize until later that there was generational trauma in my bloodline.

Let's break generational trauma out of your bloodline by saying this prayer:

 "God, I stand in the gap for all past generations in my bloodline, and I repent of any sin that opened the

spiritual door to trauma. I ask that You forgive my ancestors and cleanse my bloodline all the way back to Adam. Now I command generational trauma to be cut off my bloodline, and I declare repayment with generational blessings to come down. Restore my bloodline, Lord."

Overcoming Trauma

"Part of the process of overcoming trauma is realizing that you are now safe."

I remember trying hard to handle the control that my stepfather had over me by staying in my room. He made me stay in my room a lot. I can laugh about it now, but I survived by reading and watching movies. It helped me escape my miserable reality. I see now that this was my coping mechanism. We had a Bookmobile that would come by and deliver books. I read series such as *The Babysitters Club* and *American Girl*, and I watched movies like *The Goonies* and *The Wizard of Oz*. My stepdad was on Workmen's Compensation, so he did not work. This was another reason why I stayed in my room all day. I did not have to deal with him, and I felt safer there. I studied things like sharks and watched the movie *Jaws* because the subject fascinated me.

I was deceived in thinking this was the normal family life and dreamed of better days. When anyone goes through something traumatic over and over again, they try to find coping mechanisms that make them feel safer, and that makes life bearable for them. I realize now that my God is bigger than any trauma that has ever happened to me. You may be asking why did this happen? Why did God allow this to happen? This brings me to an important point: God did not allow this to happen! The earth became Satan's in the garden when man fell into sin. Since then, we have had to deal with demons that can and will harm us if we do not know who we are in Christ.

Right now, for anyone reading this who has had a traumatic experience, I release the breaker anointing to you for a breakthrough.

Speak this out loud with me:

"I renounce trauma from any abuse, neglect, near-death experience, unmet needs, and any other trauma that was caused in my life. Thank you, Holy Spirit, for allowing your glory to rush in and wash those memories away. Heal my soul wounds supernaturally. I choose to forgive _____ for all the things they did to me, thereby stopping access to the tormenter to hold me, prisoner."

I am not asking you to condone what they did, I am asking you to release what they did, so it cannot dictate your future. I also ask you to let go of the shame.

 **I break shame off your mind and heart for what happened and, instead, I speak honor over you. You are a person of honor, God's son, or daughter.**

I am so proud of you for having prayed this prayer! The enemy is scared of the person you are becoming, and trauma tried to fragment you and keep you from realizing who you are in Christ. I pray right now for everyone who is reading this that the Holy Spirit would comfort them in a supernatural way over the next thirty days. Thank You, Holy Spirit, for doing a divine exchange in their life.

I declare Isaiah 61:3 over you. I release hope to your heart because, as the Word says in Proverbs 13:12, "Hope deferred makes the heart sick, but a longing fulfilled is like a tree of life." Allow the peace of God to overflow your mind. I speak to your spirit, man, YOU are safe; you are safe.

Part of the process of overcoming trauma is realizing that you are now safe.

I come against any dream of fear or torment, and any familiar spirits who try to open the door for Satan to attack you again. I plead the blood of Jesus over your dreams.

I am writing all of this to help you. I wish someone—anyone—would have walked me through this process when I needed it. This way, you can spend the rest of your life making decisions out of wholeness, not from a place of woundedness.

I continued to be abused as a child. So, at the age of 12, I decided to move out and live with my dad. Soon after that, I moved quickly into an attitude of rebellion. Rebellion opens the door to witchcraft, as the Word says in 1 Samuel 15:23. I suggest that you just repent if you have already started using rebellion as a coping mechanism in your life.

Say this with me:

"Lord, please forgive me for operating in rebellion because of the trauma that has happened to me. I repent for it, and I come out of agreement with rebellion. I command any witchcraft to go back to where it may have come in as a result of my actions."

After all the control I suffered, I had no respect for authority because I viewed anyone in that position as someone who could abuse me. My flesh wanted nothing to do with anyone telling me what to do. All the while, I was yearning for authority in the right way. There is safety under correct, healthy authority. Because of the abuse, I also suffered from a deep wound of rejection. I yearned for acceptance and attention in any way that I could get them. I started having sex and doing drugs at a very young age. I used them to escape my pain and to feel loved. Yet they were all lies and deceptions from the enemy. If you have used sex as a coping mechanism, you have created ungodly soul ties. God designed sex for man and wife because the two become one flesh. The sexual act opens spiritual doors to demonic oppression when it is not in the confines of marriage.

If you've been involved in this, please say this with me:

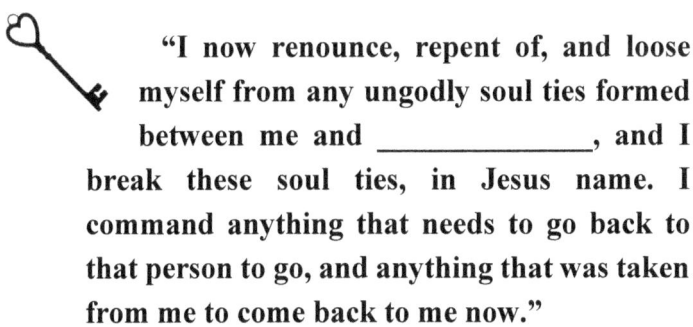

"I now renounce, repent of, and loose myself from any ungodly soul ties formed between me and _____, and I break these soul ties, in Jesus name. I command anything that needs to go back to that person to go, and anything that was taken from me to come back to me now."

It's interesting that, while I was going through this phase of my life, I still felt a deep sense that the Lord was with me and that I had a call on my life. Although it would be years before I turned to Him, He was already seeking me faithfully even then. For many years, I continued to do drugs—mostly pot—and drinking, but even then, I felt convicted. It just didn't feel right. It's surprising what humans will do for love when we were designed to receive the love of God, which fills every void in our hearts.

Many years later, skipping school and partying, I found myself pregnant at sixteen. Lost, afraid, and ashamed, I was now an outcast again. As the old saying goes, I was looking for love in all the wrong places. I could not continue to go out partying with my friends because I was pregnant. I could not hang out with my friends at school because I was going to have a baby and had to do a program called "Homebound" so I could graduate. Now I realize that this was the favor of the Lord: I got to complete the most of my 11 grade of high school at home so I could have my amazing daughter and still graduate from high school. I also recognize that it was due to the grace of God in my life that I was able to keep up with my studies during this time.

My body did not handle the pregnancy very well. I was very fatigued and exhausted around the clock, with nausea almost eleven hours a day. It was almost more than I could bear at sixteen years of age, but somehow I knew that, even on my lowest days, I was not alone. I wasn't sure how everything was going to work out, but something inside my heart always knew

God was there, even though I did not know Him. I can testify that God was pursuing me, even when I didn't know how to find him.

What was a girl to do at this point? All kinds of questions flooded my mind. I had not yet graduated, but I went from thinking about college to wondering how in the world I was going to work and take care of a baby by myself. Unfortunately, my boyfriend was not there for me during most of the pregnancy since he was in and out of jail for drugs. I had picked an unhealthy relationship because of the condition of my heart. I did not understand what love was supposed to look like and feel like.

It was very difficult for me to relate to anyone my age because my life had been so challenging. Some of it was due to attacks, and some of it was a result of my own choices because I was not prepared for the enemy's strategies. Either way, the average teen problems of *what clothes shall I wear*, or *what am I going to do this weekend* seemed so foreign to me. I realize now that Satan loved isolating me. It felt like I had nowhere to turn. In the church I attended, people never talked about abuse. I never once heard about it in a sermon, and definitely, no one talked about inner healing. There is power in having the right alignment in the Spirit—in having a community that is built around relationships that are based on friendship with the Holy Spirit. The Holy Spirit expresses who He is through you. You have a unique purpose that only you can carry out. In Jeremiah 1:5, the Word says He chose you before you were born. The Holy Spirit has to have our cooperation, and we must say "yes" to His call so that we can co-labor with Him and do the work that God has ordained for us.

I see, even as I write this, the breath of God is landing on you, and you are going to feel the wind of the Holy Spirit. Invite Him in.

Just say this:

"Holy Spirit, I invite you to fill up all the empty places in my soul."

As you feel the Holy Spirit open your mouth, and as you co-labor with Him, you will start speaking a few syllables in tongues. (Acts 19:4-6)

I declare that no weapon formed against you shall prosper. I declare the God-ordained alignments to take place in your life. I call forth the divine relationships. I declare the glory of the Lord to surround you right now. Wait to hear God's voice speaking and journal what He says to you.

Yearning for God

"Deep in my heart, I was yearning to know God."

Time passed, and I gave birth to my beautiful daughter. I was working weekends, going to high school, and raising a baby. I did the best I could with one income. I was receiving no financial support from the baby's dad. My stepmom and mom were very supportive during this time; they helped me and encouraged me. Unfortunately, my heart was still wounded, and I was operating out of brokenness.

When I graduated from high school, I was pregnant with my second child by my high school sweetheart. Sadly, he was still bound by drugs and in and out of jail. I had not yet been educated on inner healing and deliverance, so there was no revelation to me as to what was binding my boyfriend and holding him captive. I thought I could help him get better. But NO! That was not my job. It was God's job, and I should have understood that.

Even with my lack of knowledge, I knew that if he didn't stop the drugs, I would have to raise both of these kids by myself. I felt lonely because he was in jail and couldn't be there for any of the sonograms. Science says that a teenager's brain does not stop developing until age twenty-five. I am not here to debate science. With my immaturity in physical and spiritual development as a teen, I had to take one day at a time to face all the responsibilities that were on my shoulders. I was still a kid myself. If it wasn't for my hope that God was real, and that He would not forsake me, no way could I have held on?

Deep in my heart, I was yearning to know God. I asked, "Lord, are you real?" It was the deepest cry of my heart. Lost, broken, and with two kids at the age of seventeen, I was unsure of what to do next. I graduated early, but wondered, "What should I do? Should I go to college?" Then my mind would reason, "How could I? I have two kids and no child support. How would that be possible?" My stepmom helped me get a job at the hospital. I thought, "Well, this will pay rent and diapers, and at least I would have medical insurance." I worked full time while trying to make things work with the children's father. I quickly became burned out. He had no license, and I had to drive him to work an hour away, then take the kids to daycare, and then go to work for eight hours. It was exhausting carrying the responsibility and bringing in a consistent income, but God helped me do it for a while. My boyfriend asked me to marry him so we could make things right, but I refused. I knew in my heart that it was time to walk away, to protect my kids from harm. His longing for drugs increased, and he began to steal things.

I left him and moved in with my grandmother. The love of the Father came through her, even when I could not love myself. She loved me, encouraged me, and supported me. I did not receive child support and could not support myself on what I was making. I could not contribute financially to my grandmother's expenses but helped out in other ways. I was working forty hours a week or more, and it still wasn't enough. I wanted a better life and a future for my kids. Since I did not have to pay rent at the time, I decided to go to college. I had no idea what to study but decided to shadow a person doing respiratory therapy. I thought, "This is a two-year degree, and I will make pretty good money when I'm finished, so let's go for it." Money doesn't fix everything, though. What I should have been seeking was wholeness in my heart, a relationship with the Holy Spirit, and provision for my children. I still felt lost and alone—young with young children. I was working twelve-hour days on Saturdays and Sundays, and going to school Mondays through Fridays.

My grandmother was helping out with the kids and the chores. I had no idea how to be a mother, so I was relieved to have help from my grandmother. God's grace was still with me. I felt the weight of all the responsibility, yet I still desired to be nineteen or twenty years old. When I finally got a chance to see my friends and go out with them, I was looking for an escape from all the burdens and pain. I would go out drinking or dancing, but I didn't have much desire for pot because I liked being in control. I went out on a few dates when I could manage it with my crazy schedule, but I met all the wrong guys.

When you are wounded and dealing with rejection, trauma, and many other things, you draw unwholesome people to yourself. It's like a brokenness magnet. I attracted men who partied, who would lie, and who would try to hide doing drugs from me. I thought, "Man, if I could just meet the right guy, my family would be normal." What a lie from the enemy that was! I needed inner healing and deliverance. Why was this not being talked about and taught? Yet we see over and over again, in the Scriptures, where Jesus talks about the soul. Here are a few Scriptures that speak about the soul: "He heals the brokenhearted and bandages their wounds." (Psalm 147:3, NET) "For I will restore your health to you, and your wounds I will heal, declares the Lord, because they have called you an outcast." (Jeremiah 30:17, ASV) "The lord is near to the brokenhearted and saves the crushed in spirit." (Psalm 34:18, ESV) These are only three verses; there are so many more.

I finally cut all ties with the wrong guys and tried to juggle being a mom to young kids. After bathing the children and putting them to bed, I would still have up to five hours of homework to do. I knew I could not continue at this pace. It's impossible to put kids to bed, sit up until 1:00 a.m. to do homework, and then get up at 6:00 a.m. for school. I decided to do an Associate Program in three years, instead of the two-year program, to cut down on the amount of homework. This reduced my nightly homework from five hours to about two hours.

I realized that, for the sake of my kids and my health, I needed a long-term plan that I could stick with and survive. I continued going to school during the week and working on weekends. I missed my kids; it seemed like I only saw them long enough to eat dinner, give them a bath, and then put them to bed. Thank God for the servant's heart of my grandmother. She would have dinner ready for us as I walked in the door from college. It was the only way I could spend some time with the kids. What did I have to give them? I was so empty and wounded, yet I tried to love them the best I knew how. I didn't have the Father's love and acceptance flowing through me and was unable to pour out to them. All that kept me going, day and night, was the hope of a better job, to be able to provide for my kids. I wanted them to have more than what I had. Being busy does not equal freedom. I gave all I had to take care of my kids and to provide, so we could survive, but I was still bound up and BROKEN.

As the busyness continued, I was asked out on a date. This man seemed to talk about Jesus a lot. I thought, "Awesome! I have so many questions." When we were together, we would stay up late to have conversations about God. I would ask what seemed like a thousand questions. In my job at the hospital, I was trained to analyze and assess patients. But because of my analytical mind, I couldn't understand grace. I thought I had accepted Jesus as a kid, but, in my mind, it didn't seem to stick. The revelation of the full concept of that decision had not hit me yet. I thought, "How could the God of the universe love me and accept me with all my mistakes? How could He just forgive me right off the bat?" This seemed so odd to me. "How could He love me when I didn't even love myself at this point?" Every time I thought about accepting Jesus, the enemy would bring to my mind every mistake I had ever made. These included drugs, sex, and pride, just to name a few. I could not understand that a Father could love me right where I was at.

My dad had been through a lot in his life and was very wounded. I thank God for my dad, and I later found out that he was a seer and was attacked all of his life because of it. He was always curious about the supernatural because of His God-given gift. He was rejected by the church because he didn't fit in their box. He was bound up by feelings of rejection (like most prophets) and plagued by the aftermath of trauma in his own heart. Allow me to break off your trauma from sexual abuse right now.

I command trauma from sexual abuse to leave you now. Let the Holy Spirit heal every memory involving that incident. Invite Him to fill you and replace that pain. God, please raise up a standard for everyone reading this. Let peace flood inside their mind right now.

Having said all that, my dad and I did not have the best relationship because of all his pain. You cannot pour out what you don't have. Alcohol consumed my dad due to the pain of the terrible, traumatic events in his life. My dad broke the cycle of physical abuse in our family line. I must brag on him for being so courageous. All this stuff affected our relationship and made it difficult for me to understand what a father was supposed to be. My earthly dad did not have the emotional wholeness to be emotionally close to me.

Therefore, I thought, "Why would God, my heavenly dad, want to be close to me?" I now know that I was suffering from a father wound.

As you take this journey, I hope you can glean from my years of suffering and walk into your wholeness now. If you have great wounds from unmet needs with your father, forgive him and ask the Holy Spirit to heal those wounds right now, and to help you relate better to God the Father.

 **I take authority over the Spirit of neglect and command it to leave you now. Come, Holy Spirit, re-fill this reader.**

God is faithful; humans will always fail. You know that, at times, you have failed. Allow God to become your source of acceptance, love, and encouragement. He created you; therefore, he knows how to fill your empty love tank the fastest! As described in the book *The Five Love Languages*, by Gary Chapman, God can meet your needs too.

Ask the Holy Spirit to help you:

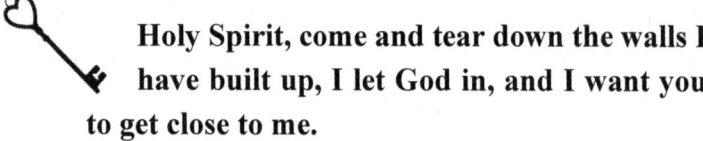
Holy Spirit, come and tear down the walls I have built up, I let God in, and I want you to get close to me.

I had a problem with this. Because of all my pain of feeling rejected and abandoned, I had built many walls up around my heart. I thought, "How can I let God in to love me as I am? What if He rejects me?" Lies from the enemy hit my mind again. The Bible says, in Psalm 139:13-14 (NIV), that God knit me together in my mother's womb. Think about that for a second! The Creator of the universe knit you together. God created you with unique qualities, talents, gifts, and assignments by knitting you together. It also says that you are "fearfully and wonderfully made." The Word goes on to talk about your destiny in verse 16. It says, "Your eyes saw my unformed body; all the days ordained for me were written in your book before one of them came to be." He has things that are ordained for you, regardless of your circumstances here on earth. God needs you, and He invites you into a relationship with Him. He wants you to understand His heart towards you, and to realize all He has created you to be.

Will you take your walls down and let God in? He yearns to heal your pain of betrayal and rejection. He yearns to show you the truth of who you really are. He believes in you and wants to help you love yourself. I pray that, as you read this, you will experience open Heaven in your life, as Jesus had in Mark 1:10, and that you will feel the Father's presence, even if it is for the very first time. There is nothing like the presence of the Father to help you tear down walls and let him speak to you.

I declare breakthrough in any generational curse that would hinder you from hearing the affirming voice of the Father.

The Bible says, in Psalm 46:10, to "be still and know that I am God."

Practice quieting yourself before the Lord and say:

"Jesus, I accept you in my life. Help me to tear down my walls and listen to what you say about me."

I pray over you that the Lord will pull down any lies about your identity and that you will have a revelation about what it means to be a son or daughter of the LIVING God.

Say this out loud:

 **"I am God-like and very good."**

God created you in His image, and that is an honor if you really think about it. He chose to make us like Himself. He could have made humans in any image, but He wanted us to be sons and daughters of His. I get so excited to know that now! I wish I had this revelation during the time I have been describing to you—my many years of woundedness. I was about as tough as they come and used to think inner healing was for wimps. I did not know that, deep down, it was the very thing that my heart needed and had been longing for most of my life.

The Process

"Jesus comes in and loves you into wholeness, but it's a process."

The wonderful man I had met was talking to me about Jesus every day. One day, we went for a drive on the parkway, and we sat down on the sidewalk and talked about Jesus for hours. I finally understood the concept of grace and accepted Jesus into my heart for real. Having a Savior who loved me was a new concept to me. For the first time in my life, all the lies had been pulled down so I could see the truth of the gospel. John 8:32 (NET) says, "And you will know the truth, and the truth will set you free." There will be a revelation of the Father as he heals your heart. You will begin to understand the greatness of his love and the personal salvation that Jesus Christ brings. John 8:36 states: "So if the Son sets you free, you will be free indeed." I pray that you will experience this verse while reading the rest of this book.

I was loved, but had not been set free and healed yet. It took longer than just one year to get all of the wounds and brokenness healed; it wasn't going to be an instant fix. Jesus comes in and loves you into wholeness, but it's a process. Unfortunately, I started dating this man. Whenever you start a relationship without first being healed emotionally through the Holy Spirit, it has a ripple effect. I had not learned to love myself yet, and no one had taught me what inner healing was and how vitally important it is. "Sozo," or complete wholeness, was never taught to me. I had received counseling before I got saved, but it didn't help one bit. Please don't misinterpret what I am saying: I believe that, for some people and situations, counseling can be very effective and is definitely needed. However, I had suffered so much that human wisdom could not help me one bit. The pain was stuffed deep down in my heart, making it difficult to keep my family together and survive.

All of the trauma and emotional scars did not disappear in counseling. There was a wound in my soul, and deliverance was needed. Oh, how I wish the church would talk about this stuff and allow the Holy Spirit to make people whole. I long to see the body of Christ free of all internal wounds. How much more effective would God's people be if they were ministering out of a place of love—a place of wholeness. That is what will create a strong and effective army for the Lord—an army that the enemy cannot attack over and over again from the open door of internal wounds in the soul—an army that is equipped to move in sync with the Lord. If you want to know more about this subject, I highly recommend *Restoring the Foundations Ministry* or *Sozo Ministry* as a reference.

The man who helped lead me to Jesus soon became my boyfriend. I graduated from college and married this man. Now, with two young kids, I went from having to go to school during the week to work the night shifts. I worked six or seven twelve-hour shifts in a row, and I would come home only long enough to go to bed, wake up, eat, and go again. I had to ask my own children for forgiveness years later for not being there for them because of my work hours. I was using my education to provide for my family, but I never saw them.

When you walk in the door and out again for weeks on end, with no date night, and you still have woundedness, it doesn't take long before your marriage suffers and ends. This only left another wound. Right in the middle of the divorce, I found out that I was pregnant, but my husband had already moved on—moved out of state—and he was not willing to work on our marriage. This was my third pregnancy that I had to go through alone. I had accepted Jesus into my heart by this point, so this time it was different for me. I pressed into the Lord all the more. I needed Him more now than ever. He was my life source, and I was inspired not to quit. I could not quit! With three kids to think about, I had to remind myself to keep going, no matter how I was feeling. I had to do what I had to do to keep working and supporting my children, despite the fact that I was falling apart on the inside. The mind and body can cope with extreme circumstances as a way to survive, even though it is not healthy. I don't recommend it at all. That is the reason I am writing this book for you. I want you to have a revelation about inner healing and deliverance for a quick turnaround in your life.

Despite all odds and the circumstances in my life at this point, despite all this woundedness and brokenness, I had a peace that surpassed all understanding. (Philippians 4:7) This was new to me! I heard the Lord tell me to name my son Kaleb Jadon, which means "God has heard and is faithful." I needed to hear this at that very moment, as a woman, pregnant and alone, leaning into the love of the Lord to help me keep going. Somehow, I always knew that if the Lord spoke to me, I could trust Him. That was the way I was wired.

I was growing in revelation of who the Lord is. When all you have ever known is performance, religion, and rules, it takes time to undo the damaging voice of religion. Religion is always about law and no love—no movement of the Holy Spirit. Religion always keeps a person bound, but a relationship with the Godhead brings total freedom. We were not designed to follow the rules for the sake of dos and don'ts. God is so much more than that. He is the lover of your soul and the lifter of your head. According to Psalm 3:3, He is your shield, your glory, and the one who restores you.

    Say it out loud with me:

 **"Lord, you are my shield around me, my glory, the One who lifts my head high."**

I said, "Okay, Lord, your hand is on me." The Bible says, in Deuteronomy 31:6 (NIV), He never leaves nor forsakes me. I was alone, pregnant, and taking care of two young kids. I was also working lots of hours, and I was in survival mode. There was no time to heal, no time to deal with anything. I had to hold it all together for the sake of my children. They needed me to provide for them. I was soon to have a baby and needed to find a place to live. The place where I had been living was way too expensive for one income. I did what most moms would do. I put my nose to the grindstone and worked all the time. I was down to one income and had a family of three, soon to be four to feed. I had no choice but to work a lot.

The wound of abandonment and rejection set in deeper. I barely had time to go to church or fellowship with like-minded believers because I had too much responsibility. Having to miss my kids' homework time and school plays because of work was disheartening to us all. I was finally able to find a two-bedroom apartment and start preparing for a new baby. At least I could breathe easier because the place was our own. I hated the fact that my kids did not have a yard to play in. They were still young— seven and six years old. My son and daughter would have to share a room, and the baby would have to be in my room, but it was ours.

At least I was now working twelve-hour day shifts instead of nights, but I was still working too much, and I had to fight for time just to help the kids with homework. I was getting home at 8:00 p.m. at night, exhausted from work and from being six months pregnant. Each day, it was becoming harder and harder. My mind would be exhausted by the time I got home. "How am I going to do this, Lord?" I kept asking. I was giving it all I had, but I had not learned to soak and lean into God's presence.

There is truth to what the Bible says in Psalm 46:10 (NET): "Stop your striving and recognize that I am God!" However, at that time, I still had no revelation of the beauty of God's manifested presence. I was living on self-effort and in my own strength—in survival mode. That's what trauma does. It keeps you going at a fast pace and keeps you in survival mode. I didn't know how to do as Jesus instructed in Matthew 11:28-30 (NET): "Come to me, all you who are weary and burdened, and I will give you rest. Take my yoke on you and learn from me, because I am gentle and humble in heart, and you will find rest for your souls. For my yoke is easy to bear, and my load is not hard to carry."

I just thought if I kept going, kept doing, God would make everything okay. Intimacy with the Lord was what I needed more than anything, but as I prayed and cried out and worshiped him, I was always going one hundred miles an hour and not releasing all my cares. I did not know how to invite the Lord into my wounds; I didn't even realize that all these internal wounds were there. All I knew was that I was too busy to even think about it. It's funny how that happens. I was now in my mid-twenties, and, for the majority of my life, I had been living with these deep wounds. Even as I type this, many years later, I am still so thankful for the Holy Spirit. He really is the comforter! I'm thankful that He did not let me continue throughout my life like that. I had some physical sickness off and on during my teenage years. I now know that this was abnormal and that it was the result of all those emotional wounds.

Finally, the day came: January 31, 2006. My son Kaleb was born! Let me tell you, that birth since I was now truly saved, was so supernatural. The Lord's presence was in the atmosphere, and His angelic hosts were there. Everything went as smoothly as possible. There were no complications, only peace. It was refreshing to me, even during that time, when I didn't yet know how to soak as Samuel did. Some Scriptures that talk about soaking include Psalm 37:7, Psalm 23:1-3, Hebrews 4:9-11, Isaiah 40:29-31, and Psalm 27:14. There are also many books you can read about entering a secret place.

So, what happened to me? I woke up in bed one day, wondering what had happened. It felt like a tornado had hit my life. I was alone with three young kids, trying to pay bills, breastfeeding, and working thirteen-hour days. But, at the end of each day, I was beyond exhausted. My kids had unmet needs, and I was getting sicker by the day. I was feeling weak, and my body was hurting all over. My kids wanted me to go to the park, throw a ball, or play a game. Little did they know it was a struggle for me just to get out of bed to go to work. I soon began to feel helpless, depressed, and full of grief. My pain level, on most days, was a ten out of ten. It hurt to walk, move, and even sleep at night. It was like living a nightmare. Each day, it felt like no vigor was in me. Trauma had opened the door to an infirmity spirit that was attacking my body, as well as many other spirits that were attacking my mind. The medical community calls what I was suffering from "fibromyalgia." My thyroid was also overactive because of the stress— probably PTSD.

I didn't realize the enemy of my soul was oppressing me. I refused to take any prescription drugs. I tried them once, and all it did was make me loopy. I thought, "How could the doctors expect me to raise kids while taking a medication like that? How could I function and be cognitive enough to raise kids, when I feel like my head is numb and cloudy because of that stuff?" I would just try to take 800 mg of ibuprofen if I had trouble moving, but even that I would not do very often. If only I had been equipped to recognize what was happening to me. If only deliverance and inner healing had been taught in the church.

Being employed in the medical field, I knew that it was not good for my organs to take even that amount of ibuprofen very often. My mind would ask, "God, is there anyone who can help me? Any doctor, chiropractor, specialist—anyone, Lord, who can give me answers and make me feel better?" I know now that all I really needed was a revelation, but, back then, all I could hear was the voice of religion. I asked myself: "Do you have unforgiveness? Are you in any sin at all?

Maybe God wants you to suffer for His glory." All of these bad thoughts kept lying to my mind! You see, I had already searched my heart about twenty times and said, "Lord, I forgive this person, and that person, and that person." Heck, it felt like I forgave people that I didn't even need to forgive, just because I wanted to search my heart thoroughly a thousand times, and just to be sure I didn't forget anyone because that was the church's most common solution. I still thought, "Surely, you need to forgive somebody."

I was trying to get the breakthrough that I so desperately needed to hold this family together. However, I had already dealt with the people I needed to forgive when I got saved. By the grace of God, he quickly helped me with forgiveness. So that was not the problem!

Next, I went down the line, asking myself: "Is there any sin in my life?" Well, that's a loaded question. I mean, the Bible says that if we even think a wrong thought about someone, it's a sin. But, nonetheless, I thought I would take this adventure and see where it would lead. I started repenting for everything. Then I would get mad at a car cutting me off in traffic, or not be patient enough with the kids for their misbehavior. One thought after another came to mind, and I would just disqualify myself from God's "good list." No matter how much I tried to modify my behavior and be good enough for Jesus to heal me, it wasn't working. Perfectionism only led me to feel even more condemned, and I was getting sicker. My energy level, most days, was a zero; my pain never eased from a level ten, and I was literally only sleeping about one to two hours a night. I needed inner healing and deliverance!

Meanwhile, I was trying to keep up with an eight-year-old little girl (whom I adored), a seven-year-old boy (who had tons of energy to RUN), and a four-month-old who only wanted breast milk and refused any other type of milk! I was waking up at 4:00 a.m. to take the kids to the babysitter, driving to work, and then working 12 hours. After work, I would have to pick up the kids, and I would not arrive home until 9:30 p.m. I would stare in my kids' faces, worrying because they had not had dinner yet, none of their homework was done, and most of their emotional needs were left unmet. I felt like a failure and slowly slipped deeper into depression. I thought if I was good enough for Jesus to heal me, but I couldn't meet my kids' needs as a mother, then what good was I? My identity was being shaken to the core, in a bad way, in a deceptive way. If only I had been disciplined and had a better understanding of my authority and my relationship with God as a child—as a beloved daughter. I did not yet realize that I was not an orphan child; I was a King's daughter.

As I look back at these very moments, I realize that this is the most important truth that can ever be revealed to you. You are a child of God, born and set apart for His purposes.

 **I bind any orphan spirit in you and command it to go.**

Now declare this:

 "I come out of agreement with any thoughts that are not God's thoughts about me."

As you read this, I declare fresh revelation to hit your eyes and mind, and for a spirit of adoption into Christ to wash over you. If you have never accepted Jesus into your heart, just ask Him to come in now. Just say, "Jesus, I acknowledge what you did on the cross for me, and I confess my sins before you. I need You to come into my life and show me what it means to be a child of God."

Open up your mind to the possibilities of what God has for you.

You see, my circumstances were not matching up with the Word of God, and, deep in my heart, I knew there was something missing. There was something I needed to understand about Jesus the Healer. As a child of God and a mother, I didn't want any of my kids to be sick. I was searching deep in my heart to know the God that I learned about in Sunday school, in that little Methodist church, when I was growing up. I had such a longing to know the very heart of God. Deep down, I had to find out whether God still heals today. I wouldn't stop until that question was answered. If it happened for some, then I knew it could happen to me. But, I was paralyzed by the tormenting question: "Is God trying to teach me something with this sickness?" In my mind, this was a possibility. But later, I learned that this was a lie.

Religion had blinded me to the truth. How cruel would I be as a parent if I taught my kids a lesson by letting them be sick for a few years? "God is not a man that he should lie." (Numbers 23:19, NET) His Word says, in John 10:10, that Jesus came to give me abundant life. But what did that mean? These were the silent questions in my heart. I felt the need to be brave, to stand and fight, and to find the truth, no matter what came at me during the jour

Walking in Wholeness

"God wants me to be His little girl, walking in wholeness."

Days came and went. I remained exhausted with chronic pain and fatigue, going from one doctor to the next, trying to figure out why I was in so much pain, unable to sleep at night, and very anxious. My heart started racing uncontrollably at night. Looking back, I realize that the enemy was trying to take me out, but I did not know that at the time. At one point, my heart rate went up to more than 150 beats per minute while I was sleeping. For all of the nonmedical people out there, it should be lower than 100 while sleeping, usually in the 70s. They referred me to a cardiologist who ran some tests. He found nothing wrong, but it kept happening. If only I understood spiritual authority back then.

I lay in my bed wide awake, mad that I couldn't sleep, and somewhat despondent because I knew I had to wake up at 4:00 a.m. to work a fourteen-hour day the next day. Then, I had a vision! I was half awake and half asleep. Suddenly, I saw someone in a white gown. It was so beautiful! It was long and bright and ruffled at the bottom. I thought, "Wow, who is that?" Amazed by the glory and glow of the gown, I looked at her face to see who it was. I was shocked. It was me! My face was glowing with the glory of God, and I had a huge sword in my hand. It seemed to be so natural. Then, as my mouth opened, strange, unfamiliar words began to come out of my mouth. I had received the gift of speaking in tongues! My voice got louder and louder, and while I was praying in tongues, I felt great power come out of my mouth. As I was speaking, I could feel the power of Satan get weaker and weaker as my voice got stronger and stronger. What I saw with my eyes was a powerful, mighty warrior. I had not even known she was there. I was mesmerized by the power and strength she had. God was showing me who I was. The real me—a mighty warrior woman. I had always been a very visual person, so He spoke to me in a way I could clearly understand. Then, bam, all of a sudden, I snapped out of the vision and woke up. WOW! I was breathing rapidly and trying to take it all in. I guess, at that very moment, God knew I needed to see who I really was and the authority I had as a believer. Unfortunately, I didn't get that revelation right away, but this vision helped me to continue to seek the Lord for understanding. All of a sudden, I could see Jesus touch my thyroid, and it was healed, and someone prayed for the fibromyalgia and all the pain left. Praise God! I am not here to glorify the sickness. I am here to worship the healer, Jesus. Jesus Christ is the same yesterday and today and forever," according to Hebrews 13:8.

If you are suffering from an illness, then I pray that, as you read this in your sickbed, God will give you an encounter, just as John the Revelator had, so you will see who you are and who He is. I declare your spiritual eyes to be opened now.

Keep pressing on; keep seeking! "He is a rewarder of those who diligently seek Him." (Hebrews 11:6, NKJV) Let this verse encourage your heart. Put it on your mirror, in your car, and in your kitchen.

Speak this out loud over your heart:

"Thank you, Father, that I have the faith to please you, and I believe that you are a rewarder of those who diligently seek You."

Lord, please give revelation that will flood the heart of your dear child who is reading this book.

Think about this: What if all those wounds that I have talked about in this book could have been closed, healed, and dealt with earlier? All the rejection I had experienced, all the trauma, shock, betrayal, neglect, shame, fear, control, and this list goes on and on. God wants to touch your soul wounds TODAY. These soul wounds were an open the door to the enemy. He was able to come and wreak havoc on my life because my wounds were not healed until much later.

To be honest, I was such a general in the attitude of my heart. Smith Wigglesworth was called one of God's generals. I love Smith Wigglesworth and his gift of faith. I thought that inner healing was for wimps because it was not the gift of faith. I did not want to slow down long enough to allow God to heal my wounds. I thought, "Inner healing—yuck, Lord!" My heart's cry was more like "Let me run, Lord, and take regions for You by faith," not knowing that the inner man had to be Sozo' to wholeness first. I now realize that healing of the heart is necessary in order to walk in total fullness and to carry out any gifting to its maximum potential to impact others. I had to repent and ask God to forgive me for the pride of thinking I could do it on my own. I wanted to go and enforce God's kingdom and wished God would just take all the pain away in one fell swoop so that I could be about my Father's business. I continued to walk with the Lord daily, learning more about who He is and what He has called me to do.

One day, the Lord spoke to me and said, "If I can heal the nations, what kind of God would I be if I didn't heal you?" Well, what can you say to that, except, "Yes, Lord, I repent for doubting You!" I was stunned by how much He valued and loved me. Yes, He wants us to do kingdom work. Yes, He wants us to step out and use our gifts. And yes, He wants us to prevail, take ground, and plunder territories. However, He also wants me to be His little girl, walking in wholeness, and knowing about the precious gift of His anointing for inner healing. As the Father healed the wounds inside of me, I felt the Holy Spirit literally rip out chunks of infected areas from my soul.

I understand that not everyone feels things in the spirit realm. You may not feel anything as you receive your healing. I am just telling you how the Holy Spirit healed me. I felt the pain of each experience, one by one. I had to cry the pain out and release it, and I would feel Him pull the infected thing out in chunks and wash the wound, and then re-fill me afresh with His love and anointing. This happened within the span of about a year, and issues were dealt with layer after layer. I look back now and realize it was the grace of God upon my life that allowed me to slow down and get intimate with the Father about the issues that needed to be addressed. The Holy Spirit eliminated all my spiritual wounds. It felt like chunks of pus coming out of me. I cried as He ripped them out, one by one. It was a process. I literally felt things physically break off me; I released the pain, and then He refilled me.

When you have suffered many things, your situation can leave you in survival mode. Working seventy hours a week and taking care of kids by yourself is sometimes necessary, but it involves a lot of activity, and there is great potential for burnout. When you are burned out, sometimes wounds can be ignored just to keep the ship afloat. After my heavenly Father transformed me, I could see how common this burnout is for women. We have the nurturing nature to give, but we have to be transformed and filled with God's Spirit to give out of wholeness and with effectiveness.

My Savior had seen me struggle long enough. I am so grateful that He never leaves us nor forsakes us (Hebrews 13:5), and that His promise to us is that "He heals the brokenhearted and binds up their wounds." (Psalm 147:3, NKJV) Looking back, I can see His faithfulness. Spiritual doors needed to be closed so I could be in a safe place (see Restoring the Foundations).

I am now full of health and enjoy the process of walking with God in obtaining more of John 10:10. " The thief comes only to steal and kill and destroy; I have come that they may have life, and have it more abundant" (NIV). I am now in partnership with the Holy Spirit to walk in my God-ordained destiny. If Holy Spirit walked me through this process, he could walk you through it as well. Let me extend this invitation to you:

If you are called to go to the nations, as the Word promises, "Ask me, and I will give you the nations as your inheritance" (Psalm 2:8, NET), you should not go out with spiritual doors open in your life when you will be facing opposition in other lands. As I am writing this, I see the Lord releasing mantles over people that read this now, for inner healing and for the nations.

> **Lord, I declare for the ones that are willing to go for you, that the mantle will fall on them now, and You will send them to the ends of the earth. Thank you, Lord, that you will take them through a season in which You will bind up their wounds and prepare them, and that grace will be upon their lives during this time. I declare dunamis power to wash over their soul right now.**

You might ask yourself, "What would my life be like without this inner pain, without the depression, and with nothing pulling me down?" Maybe you're on the opposite side of the fence. Maybe you are the offender who has hurt someone. You are asking God, "How can you love me? I have done so many terrible things, awful things that I am not proud of." An old saying goes: "Hurt people hurt people," and there is truth to that. There may be things you wish to erase from your life and change in yourself—things you are glad that no one knows but God. This is the amazing thing about Him. He sees what you have done, and yet He still loves you! The Bible says, in Isaiah 1:18 (NIV), "Though your sins are like scarlet, they shall be as white as snow; though they are red as crimson, they shall be like wool." It's time to forgive yourself and let the Lord minister to you.

> **I declare grace over you right now to forgive yourself and to let go of the past.**

Put your hand on your heart and say,

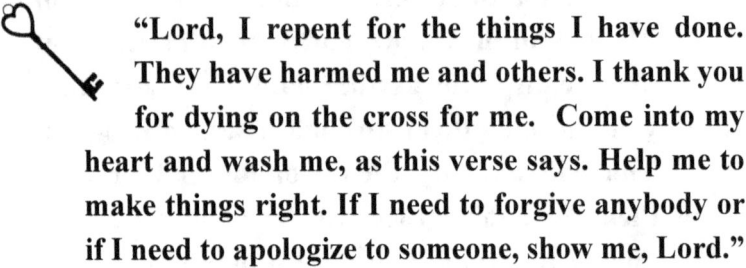
"Lord, I repent for the things I have done. They have harmed me and others. I thank you for dying on the cross for me. Come into my heart and wash me, as this verse says. Help me to make things right. If I need to forgive anybody or if I need to apologize to someone, show me, Lord."

If tears need to be released, let them flow. You are not weak for crying. Jesus wept also. It cleanses the soul, and the Word says, in Psalm 56:8 (NLT), "You keep track of all my sorrows. You have collected all my tears in your bottle. You have recorded each one in your book."

Sometimes forgiving yourself can be the hardest step, but it is a necessary step in order to move to where you want to be in life. You don't want to carry your wounds over into your marriage, into parenting your kids, or into your job. Forgiving yourself will help you be a BETTER you. It will allow you to put healthy boundaries on your own actions from this day forward.

The Word says, in James 1:5 (NKJV), "If any of you lacks wisdom, let him ask of God, who gives to all liberally and without reproach, and it will be given to him." You may not have had a good example in your life to teach you how to be a mother or father, to have a good work ethic, or to be a great, supportive spouse. God is willing to come alongside you and help you transition into who you want to become. It is a choice daily.

You can ask Him to show you how you can do things differently. Listen to God and journal what He shows you. Renew your mind with the Word of God. Maybe you have been through a divorce, and you want to learn from what happened. Take a notepad and journal the things that the Lord wants to help you overcome. Bringing these issues before the Lord and asking for wisdom is healthy, once you have allowed Him to heal the pain of the past. We are all being transformed into His likeness; that takes time, and it takes the right decisions. Simply having chosen to read this book shows that you are willing to make some changes in your life.

I can see now in the Spirit that, as some of you do the steps on this page, God is going to show you, gently and lovingly, some areas in which He is going to partner with you to make your relationships better and your work better. Be willing and open to hear and reflect on what He wants to show you.

If need be, find an accountability partner— someone you can trust, and tell them:

 **"I am going to be brave and invite God to heal every soul wound that is left in me. I am making this change in my life this week. Can you call me once a week to see how I am doing with this?"**

Some weeks may go better than others, but be open and honest with your accountability partner, so he or she can pray with you. Some people may not feel ready to take this step. That's okay! The Word says that Jesus is a friend who sticks closer than a brother. Tell Him everything!

I may not have been through exactly what you have been through. My wounds may have been different than yours, but I know the Healer. I invite you to know Him as well. He can't wait to make Himself real to you! I have prayed for everyone who reads my story—that God will meet you at your point of need—that you will walk in His grace and lean into Him as He restores your soul. I have provided some Scriptures to speak over yourself:

Declarations to speak over your soul:

"**Thank you, Lord! I declare, according to Psalm 34:18, that you are near to my broken heart, and you will save my crushed Spirit and heal my wounds.**"

"**Thank you, Lord! I declare, according to John 8:32, that I know the truth of who You are, and the truth is setting me free.**"

"**Thank you, Lord! According to Psalm 147:3, You heal the brokenhearted, and You bind up my wounds.**"

"According to Psalm 30:2, Lord, I have cried out for help, and you have healed me."

"According to Psalm 34:19, many are the afflictions of the righteous, but the Lord delivers me from them all."

From Victim to Victory

"God wants us to go from Victim to Victory, our soul, and spirit."

This will be an expansion of my book in the future.

Closing Thoughts

It is my prayer as you read this book that it has been a blessing to your life. I pray if you have any health issues that Jesus the healer can heal you of your condition now and forevermore.

CHAPTER ONE NOTES

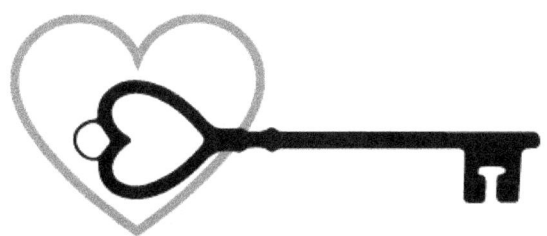

CHAPTER TWO NOTES

_____
_____
_____
_____
_____
_____
_____
_____
_____
_____
_____
_____

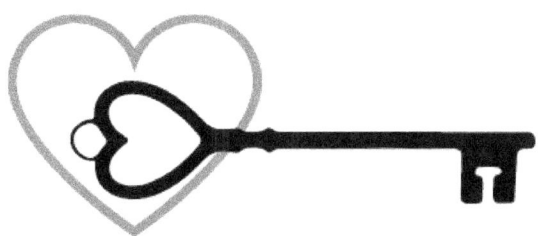

CHAPTER THREE NOTES

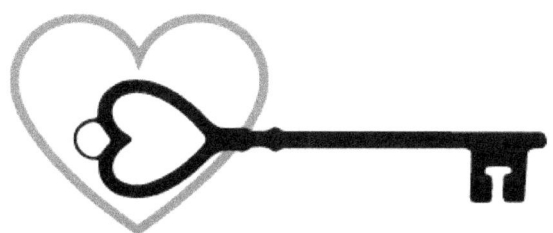

CHAPTER FOUR NOTES

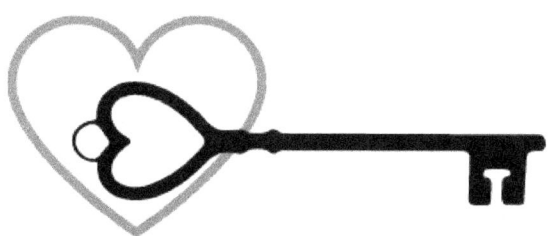

CHAPTER FIVE NOTES

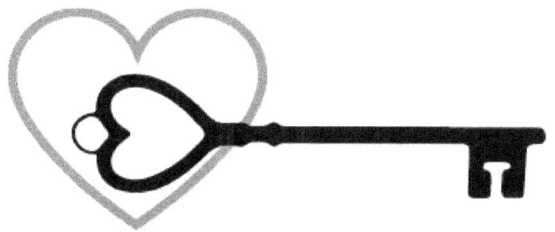

CHAPTER SIX NOTES

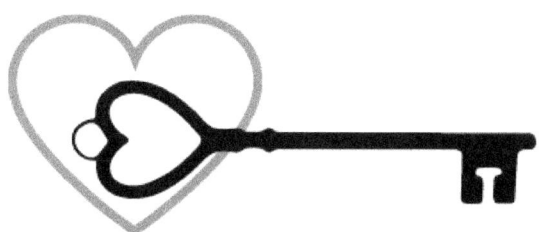

Notes

Chapter 1: What Is Discerning of Spirits?

1. https://en.wikipedia.org/wiki/Discernment

2. Jennifer Eivaz, Seeing The Supernatural, chapter. 2 (Grand Rapids, Michigan. *Chosen Books*, 2017]

Chapter 2: Help, What Do I Feel?

3. Gateway to my Miracle by April Stutzman [Self Published.: April Stutzman, 2018]

   Ebook: https://amzn.to/3aLcRSI

   Paperback: https://amzn.to/38G26P2

   Large Print: https://amzn.to/3pto5zy

   Hardback: https://amzn.to/3rwOqgO

   Audio book: https://amzn.to/2X7knzn

About the Author

April Stutzman is co-founder with her husband Richard Stutzman of Kingdom Flame Ministries. She is a powerful deliverance minister and prophetic voice. April shares the heart of the Father to see people walk into wholeness and activated in their destiny. Currently, April and Richard are equipping the body of Christ through webinars and meetings. They love to activate people in healing, prophetic, and deliverance ministry.

To find out more about April and her ministry, you can visit her online:

Website: https://www.kingdomflameministries.com/

About the Author

Youtube: April Stutzman Glory Stories

https://www.youtube.com/GloryStoriesbyAprilStutzman

Youtube: April Stutzman – Kingdom Decree's

https://www.youtube.com/channel/UCDLLFs3ATuzsMt-4UG2At7Q

Other Sites:

Youtube: Kingdom Flame Ministries Channel

Youtube:

https://www.youtube.com/KingdomFlameMinistries

Here are other podcast Feeds to Glory Stories:

Apple Podcast:

Google Podcast:

Spotify:

Stitcher:

Amazon Music:

Breaker:

About the Author

For more information, check these links below!

Web: kingdomflameministries.com

Youtube: Kingdom Flame Ministries

YouTube: Glory Stories by April Stutzman

Facebook: Kingdom Flame Ministries

Instagram: @kingdomflameministries

Other Accounts that you can follow me.

Twitter: @bluizzforchrist

Periscope: @bluizzforchrist

Instagram: iamaprilstutzman

Kingdom Flame Ministries

PO Box 4022

Clovis, CA, 93613

More Powerful Resources from April Stutzman

More Powerful Resources

So I am a discerner, now what? Maybe that was your question as you picked up this book. Perhaps you are more mature in discernment and surprised that someone has written about it, but you are reading it out of curiosity. Either way, the Holy Spirit is going to meet you where you are! Holy Spirit has something amazing in store for you to help you navigate this gift. I feel His heart on it. Many discerners have had the gift since birth but have been unsure of what they carry. They have been misunderstood, isolated, and rejected.

I don't mean to dishonor this amazing gift from God, but I have to say it has taken me through the school of hard knocks. I believe that everyone who carries this gift wants to give up at some point. At different stages, they have wanted to lay it down and walk away. Even now, there are days when I think those thoughts. It's the very reason I wrote this book. I want to share some of the processes it takes to walk in this gifting, and I hope to encourage you and come alongside you as you grow. I love you for being brave enough to pick up this book. It shows your desire to grow your gift. That desire is the stepping stone to your higher level because the Holy Spirit will impart to you as you read.

You can copy and paste or click on Ebook link to

check out this awesome book.

Ebook: https://amzn.to/38xoREw
Paperback: https://amzn.to/2WQca2o
Large Print: https://amzn.to/36GsXKq
Hardback: https://amzn.to/30gwI5S
Audio-book: https://amzn.to/3pGCloA
Amazon CD Book:
https://amzn.to/3dyEZtH

Endorsements

If you are one seeking to be mentored in the things of the Spirit, the good news is you hold in your hand the priceless personal insights of one who has gone before you. In this book, April Stutzman reveals her very personal journey of discovery into the Discerning of Spirits. Not many people are prepared to share what you will read here for fear of being ridiculed, thought strange, or a misfit. However, if you have ever picked up thoughts that were not your own, received unexplainable feelings on a certain part of your body, or sensed or seen angels, then it is likely you were operating in the discerning of spirits. April provides wisdom in how she learned to navigate these experiences. The sad truth is many misunderstand these glimpses into the world of spirits around them and consequently fail to reach the fullness of their spiritual potential. Discerning of spirits is a complimentary gift, and for that reason, it is often overlooked. However, this gift of the Holy Spirit enhances and fine-tunes all the other gifts, including deliverance, counsel, dream interpretation, and the delivery of prophecy. This is a timely and easy-to-read journey of discovery that will add years of experience and broaden your personal understanding into the multi-faceted voice of God's Spirit.

Adrian Beale and Adam F Thompson
Authors of The Divinity Code to Understanding your Dreams and Visions
thedivinitycode.org

As the need for discernment increases in this hour, any are becoming aware they carry this gifting of discerning of spirits. The Chronicles of A Discerner is a great book that introduces, breaks down, and gives articulation to this gift. This a great tool for any level, but especially those are stepping into the gifting of discerning of spirits. Those growing in this gift will gain greater confidence and gain a greater assurance they're not alone in this gifting. It's normal!

Madeline James, founder of Madeline James Ministries, and author of Unlocking

Your Prophetic Voice

It would be difficult to imagine a better moment in history for a book on the subject of discerning of spirits. With the current seemingly continual conflict between political ideologies, economic systems, gender identities and identity politics, sexual morays, and the pervasive role of government in every area of life, we must be able to see the world through God's eyes and act decisively and confidently by His grace.

Traditional mindsets will not show us how to live in these chaotic times. We must know God's will and to be able to articulate it against every vain philosophy and worldly orientation to be overcomers.

I heartily recommend April Stutzman's book, The Chronicles of a Discerner, as a helpful guide through the confusing maze of modern demonic agendas that besiege today's professing Christians at every turn.

Joan Hunter Author/Healing Evangelist

host Miracles Happen TV show

April Stutzman has written a book about discernment that is not a theological dissertation but birthed from the fires of trial. God has raised up his daughter as a prophetic voice to impart to the nations of the world. This teaching comes from many personal battles that she has fought and won. I heard a minister say that the Word of God is not on trial; because the Word of the Lord will try us like the Word tried Joseph before he became prime minister of the entire world. This is the work that you hold in your hand....a life that is being tried through the gift of discernment. This gift will deliver us from death as we yield to the Holy Ghost. April Stutzman has this assignment as a prophetic deliverer to help free the people of God from demonic bondages. This book will help you understand pitfalls and principles as the gift of discernment is developed through usage. This book will enlighten and validate your walk in the Spirit as the gift of discernment increases in the glory.

Apostle Clinton C. Baker Co-Founder of Valiant

Ministries International, Inc.

Chronicles of a Discerner is a practical yet powerful guide that will help you gain an understanding of the gift of discernment in greater depths. April walks you through her own personal journey of this unique gift and shares how she grew "spiritual muscles" to carry the weight of what the Lord has shown her over the years of cultivating a beautiful and personal relationship with the Holy Spirit. April also helps you to navigate what you may already be experiencing or will experience in your own life and calling. Not only will this book give you language, but it will also stir up a hunger to go after an intimate relationship with the Spirit of the Living God and to partner with Him in everything that you discern. Get ready to learn how to walk out this gift in the love of the Father!

Teryn Yancey,

Co-Founder of Glory Culture International

I highly recommend April's new book, The Chronicles of a Discerner. April is an extraordinary discerner and uses extravagant wisdom in discerning. The tips April shares in this book are a blessing to all who read it. Teaching any level discerner to stretch and grow. Pulling you to a higher level of discerning of spirits in the days we are living in.

Joanna Beck Ministries

Wow...this book is an excellent simple read!! April's experiences were the Holy Spirits soil for His seeds to grow and mature her in this gift. She is precise and teaches along the way, as she navigates through her journey. This is an anointed and very necessary book in the hour we are living in. I highly recommend it!!

Constance J. Bounds

Gods Eagles Ministry

As you read Chronicles of a Discerner or study under April Stutzman in any of her classes, you will have your senses trained in discernment as the Word of God encourages every believer to do. She does not mince words or hold back – she lays it out straight and encourages every believer to come up higher!

April writes, "I hope to help you recognize your gift and how to partner with God in it. I want you to know you are not crazy when you see or sense what others do not!" It is refreshing to read a book that is not only instructional and empowering but also transparent and easy to read. Chronicles of a Discerner is filled with prayers and impartation, as well as clear steps to navigate this powerful gift.

It is my great pleasure to recommend Chronicles of a Discerner by April Stutzman.

."...He gives someone else the ability to discern whether a message is from the Spirit of God or from another spirit." (1 Cor. 12:10 NLT)

Pastor Jodi Ahrens-Ferguson

Co-Founder of Warriors Heart Ministry

YouTube: Signs Following with JC

¡Este libro está disponible en formato electrónico y en rústica!

Freedom Sessions-Internal Healing of the Soul!

My husband and I enjoy ministering internal healing through Freedom Sessions online through Zoom or Google Meet Video. These sessions are generally two-hours long. Christ came to set the captives free, and we have received this mantle from the Lord. Our desire is to see each one walking in their God-given destiny. Over time wounds happen, cycles take place, and generational sin affects the bloodline. When we appropriate the power of the cross on the DNA, we bring victory to generational bloodlines for the purpose of carrying the glory. It is our most profound passion to see bloodlines restored to God's original intent.

Following is a list of a few of the areas we have ministered to. There are many more.

Molestation

Rape

Trauma

Freemasonry

Abuse

History of cultism

Rejection

Orphan

Abandonment

Anger

Sexuality

Fear

Demons

Attack in Dreams

We have ministered to a lot of prophets and prophetic people by the mantle of the Lord. It is highly significant, as an Oracle of God, to deal with all issues of the heart so that they cannot contaminate your voice. The lens that we see and hear the Father through is related to our foundation. When we walk through the process of healing, we begin to make our foundation reliable in Jesus Christ.

More Powerful Resources

Click on this QR and go to our website:

If you would consider and pray to sow into our ministry that would be awesome. Here are a few ways to give or our website.

Personal Testimonies

I would love to thank Richard and April for their love and care. When I met them and began a prayer, I felt like a family automatically.

I've received so much breakthrough without even trying to do so. My family has also seen healing through my healing!

KB

The most freeing thing I have experienced through the freedom sessions is the space to be open and discuss my "issues" and not feel judged. To understand, I'm not crazy, and there is a solution. Jesus cares about every single little detail of my life (thoughts, emotions, and experiences), and I can fully trust and believe in Him to set me free from anything that hinders me from moving forward into my destiny!

Christy

Here is one of the testimonies of an SRA person that we have ministered too.

Some of us go through life with problems that we cannot seem to get over. We know somehow that there are issues that need to be resolved but have no idea where to start. I am so thankful for April and Richard for their diligence in studying and becoming knowledgeable in areas that are so horrible that most people don't want to deal with them. Because of their Freedom Sessions, I am experiencing freedom in areas that I thought I would never be free in. I have hope, I have peace, and more and more, I am walking in my true identity. I am extremely thankful to my Savior and Deliverer and for His servants, April and Richard, for ministering freedom to the captives. There is hope!

Anonymous

My sessions with April and Richard have been transformative on many levels, some of which I am confident I haven't even seen the fullness of yet. They do incredible work in the spirit realm! I've been able to both learn from their methods as well as simply receive healing and deliverance through their prayers. Most importantly, my sessions with them have increased my awareness of my authority and have grown me in confidence of who the Lord has created me to be. Their prophetic discernment has offered a lot of confirmation and encouragement to me. I've felt fear being dismantled, generational strongholds being shaken, and self-doubt and self-condemnation dissolve. Thank you, Jesus!

Love you guys, **Allie**

April's freedom sessions have been incredible!! I've had generational curses broken off. I feel more sensitive to the leading of the Holy Spirit and increase in the presence of the Lord!! Also, my Christian mother was tormented by demons for years!! This torment was removed through April being a seer by the power of the Holy Spirit!! She's been set free from years of what I thought were mental problems, but she saw it in the Spirit! Wow, these were real demonic activities operating in my mother's life so thankful for April and her husband, Richard!!!

Hal

Contact Information for Freedom Session-Internal Healing.

Email: info@kingdomflameministries.com

Website: www.kingdomflameministries.com/deliverance

We have 2 hours of session rates.

We wanted you to know that my ebook is available on many platforms including these: Apple, Amazon, Kindle, Google Play, Kobo, Scribd, Angus, Nook, Barnes & Noble, Booktopia, 24 Symbols, Bidi, Leamos, Periego, Digital PDF Ebook located on our website!

More Powerful Resources

Kingdom Flame T-Shirts Website Design and other items for sale!
---

https://kingdomflame.threadless.com/

More Powerful Resources

Kingdom Flame Ministries Resource Center!

https://www.kingdomflameministries.com/resources

Introduction to Deliverance

1. What is deliverance
2. Who needs deliverance
3. Reasons why deliverance is needed
4. How do I start the process of deliverance
5. Basics of beginner's deliverance ministry
6. Impartation and Activation

Teaching by April Stutzman
www.kingdomflameministries.com
@April Stutzman 2020 All Rights Reserved
MP3 (Download) - CD-Audio - DVD Video

Introduction to Deliverance

Topics includes:
- What is deliverance
- Who needs deliverance?
- Reasons why deliverance is needed
- How do I start the process of deliverance?
- Basics of beginner's deliverance ministry
- Impartation & Activation

Preview of Webinar: https://youtu.be/lY3yrdjGxFk

More Powerful Resources

> **6 Thing's that hinder's your Prophetic Flow**
> 1. Discussion on what the bible says about prophecy
> 2. What are 6 thing's that can hinder your prophetic voice
> 3. What are prophetic acts
> 4. Prayer and impartation
> 5. Activations
>
> *2 Hour's Session*
>
> **Teaching by April Stutzman**
> www.kingdomflameministries.com
> @April Stutzman 2020 All Rights Reserved
> MP3 (Download) - CD-Audio - DVD Video

6 Things that Hinders your Prophetic Flow

Topics includes:
- Discussion on what the Bible says about prophecy
- What are prophetic acts
- What are 6 things that can hinder your prophetic voice
- Prayer and impartation

Preview of Webinar: https://youtu.be/TfsIk9BBeLg

More Powerful Resources

Carving a realm In Joy

1. What is true Joy?
2. Why is Joy a Weapon?
3. How do we walk in joy during the midst of hard places?
4. How to allow Joy to impact those around us?
5. How did David express Joy?
6. What re some of the invaluable lessons of Joy?
7. Is Joy a Weapon?

8 Hour's Session

Teaching by April Stutzman

www.kingdomflameministries.com
MP3 (Download) - CD Audio - DVD Video

Carving a realm In Joy

Topics includes:
- What is true, Joy?
- How do we walk in joy during the midst of hard places?
- Why is Joy a weapon?
- How to allow Joy to impact those around us?
- Is Joy a weapon?
- How did David express Joy?
- What are some of the Invaluable lessons of joy?

Preview of Webinar: https://youtu.be/LTkFktWvqCk

More Powerful Resources

Prophetic Equipping

1. Prophetic ministry verses the office of a prophet
2. Common attacks that try to hinder the prophetic flow in your life
3. Overcoming hinderances in the prophetic
4. Prophetic ministry times with Q & A
5. What is a seer prophet?

11 Hour's Session's
Teaching by April Stutzman

www.kingdomflameministries.com
MP3 (Download) - CD Audio - DVD Video

Prophetic Equipping

Topic includes:

- Prophetic ministry verses the office of a prophet
- Frequent attacks that try to hinder the prophetic flow in your life
- Overcoming hindrances in the prophetic
- Prophetic ministry times with Q and A
- Prophetic activation
- What is a seer prophet?

Preview of Webinar: https://youtu.be/yWkhI81Z-aI

More Powerful Resources

Dream Interpretation
1. Interpreting Other People's Dreams
2. The Basics - What does the bible say about dreams?
3. Type of Dreams (warning, revelation, etc.)
   Source of Dreams (God / not God)
4. Dream Symbols & Tools & Interpretative Strategies

Teaching by April and Jodi Ferguson

9 Hour's Session's

www.kingdomflameministries.com
MP3 (Download) - CD Audio - DVD Video

Dream Interpretation

Topics includes:
- The Basics – what does the Bible say about dreams?
- Type of Dreams (warning, revelation, etc.) & Source of Dreams (God / not God)
- Dream Symbols & Tools & Interpretative Strategies
- Interpreting Other People's Dreams

Preview of Webinar: https://youtu.be/mbEioaQmejY

More Powerful Resources

Internal Healing of the Soul

1. Abandonment / Abuse
2. Orphan Spirit
3. Trauma / Fear/ PTSD
4. Betrayal / Offense
5. Unforgiveness / Suicide
6. Restfulness / Bitterness
7. Impartation and Ministry times

9 Hour's Session

Teaching by April and Patricia Doty
www.kingdomflameministries.com
MP3 (Download) - CD Audio - DVD Video

Internal Healing of the Soul

Topic includes:
- Abandonment - Abuse
- Orphan Spirit
- Trauma - Fear - PTSD
- Betrayal - Offences
- Unforgiveness - Suicide
- Restfulness - Bitterness
- Impartation and ministry times

Preview of Webinar: https://youtu.be/fnSOSgtH06A

More Powerful Resources

Discerning of Spirits

1. Discerning human spirit
2. Discerning the angels
3. What is discernment and why do I need it
4. Discrening the fallen demonic Angels
5. Discerning human spirit
6. Discerning the fallen demonic Angels
7. Pitfalls of discerning
8. Impartation and Q & A sessions

8 Hour's Session
Teaching by April and Patricia Doty
www.kingdomflameministries.com
MP3 (Download) - CD Audio - DVD Video

Gifts of Discerning of Spirits

Topics includes:
- What is discernment, and why do I need it?
- Discerning Human Spirit
- Discerning the Angels
- Discerning the fallen demonic Angles
- Pitfalls of discerning -
- Impartation and Q and A sessions

Preview of Webinar: https://youtu.be/EXQuFIMwVIY

More Powerful Resources

When you have a second to leave a review on the Amazon website, we would appreciate it. It also helps the ranking for my book, so others would be encouraged to buy it.

Please click or copy the link below and leave a review. Nallie, our youngest daughter, would appreciate it as well. Bow Wow!

Amazon.com/review/create-review?&asin=1954062001

Amazon.com/review/create-review?&asin=1735175196

Blessing, *April*

More Powerful Resources

Audio books are on Apple, Amazon, Audible, Kobo, Google Play, Nook, BAM, Audiobooks, Audiobooksnow, Bol, Booktopia, Chirp, Bookbeat, and Ubook! CD Audible Available on our Website!

Free Audio Preview of Chapter 2

https://www.youtube.com/watch?v=NlNbKQIyUtg

More Powerful Resources

Audio books are on Apple, Amazon, Audible, Kobo, Google Play, Nook, BAM, Audiobooks, Audiobooksnow, Bol, Booktopia, Chirp, Bookbeat, and Ubook! CD Audible Available on our Website!

Free Audio Preview of Chapter
https://youtu.be/RRfgCBOj7w4

More Powerful Resources

Audio books are on Apple, Amazon, Audible, Kobo, Google Play, Nook, BAM, Audiobooks, Audiobooksnow, Bol, Booktopia, Chirp, Bookbeat, and Ubook! CD Audible Available on our Website!

Free Audio Preview of Chapter 1:

https://youtu.be/GKoMvvmfl8Q

Prayer for Impartation

I declare and decree over you right now any generational curses of infirmity or affliction we just cut the cord of that inequity at this repent on behalf of your ancestral line or just command all spirits of affliction all spirits of infirmity up and out of their body in the name of Jesus Christ I just released the healing power of God over every cell every tissue every muscle fiber right now I just declare in decree creative order right now by the power of the Holy Spirit over the RNA over the DNA in the name of Jesus Christ

In Jesus Mighty name,

Invite April to Speak at your Next Event

April Stutzman is a powerful and anointed speaker and minister. She is an equipper, a prophetic trainer, and carries a strong inner-healing and deliverance mantle. If you would like to have April speak at your event, please send an email with requested dates and times to.

info@kingdomflameministries.com.

Topics Include:

Prophetic Equipping

Carving a Realm of Joy Discerning of Spirits

Dream Interpretation

Introduction to Deliverance

Internal Healing of the Soul

6 things that will hinder your prophetic flow

www.ingramcontent.com/pod-product-compliance
Lightning Source LLC
Chambersburg PA
CBHW071354080526
44587CB00017B/3097